Amelia Earhart
More than a Flier

written by
Patricia Lakin

illustrated by
Alan and Lea Daniel

Aladdin

New York   London   Toronto   Sydney   Singapore

For Jennifer Klonsky: A *shaineh maideleh*,
and *balebatisheh* editor who makes my books take flight.
—P. L.

For Pat and Denis, fliers both. —A. D. and L. D.

First Aladdin edition June 2003
Text copyright © 2003 by Patricia Lakin
Illustrations copyright © 2003 by Alan and Lea Daniel

ALADDIN PAPERBACKS
An imprint of Simon & Schuster Children's Publishing Division
1230 Avenue of the Americas, New York, NY 10020

Designed by Lisa Vega
The text of this book was set in Century Old Style.

Printed in the United States of America
2 4 6 8 10 9 7 5 3 1

Library of Congress Cataloging-in-Publication Data
Lakin, Pat.
Amelia Earhart : more than a flier / written by Patricia Lakin ; illustrated by Alan and Lea Daniel.
— 1st Aladdin Paperbacks ed.
p. cm. — (Ready-to-read stories of famous Americans)
Summary: Profiles Amelia Earhart, who was the first woman to fly solo across the Atlantic Ocean,
and who disappeared during her attempt to become the first woman to fly around the world.
ISBN 0-689-85575-3 (pbk.) — ISBN 0-689-85576-1 (library ed.)
1. Earhart, Amelia, 1897–1937—Juvenile literature. 2. Women air
pilots—United States—Biography—Juvenile literature. 3. Air
pilots—United States—Biography—Juvenile literature. [1. Earhart,
Amelia, 1897–1937. 2. Air pilots. 3. Women—Biography.] I. Daniel,
Alan, 1939– ill. II. Daniel, Lea, ill. III. Title. IV. Series.
TL540.E3 L34 2003
629.13'092—dc21

2002014932

Chapter 1
Independent Amelia

1897–1907

1891	Basketball invented by James Naismith
1900	*The Wonderful Wizard of Oz* is published
1903	Teddy bear toys appear (Named after President Teddy Roosevelt)

Amelia Earhart is America's most famous female pilot. When she was a little girl, the only thing flying high in the sky were birds. Airplanes hadn't been invented yet! But she dreamed of flying in this poem she wrote.

I watch the birds flying all day long
And I want to fly too

Amelia was born in Atchison, Kansas, on July 24, 1897. When Amelia was growing up, girls did not play sports, wear pants, wear their hair short, or plan to have careers. Girls were expected to get married, have children, and stay at home.

But Amelia did not want to follow those rules. She was an independent girl who loved adventure and excitement. She wanted the same opportunities that were automatically given to boys. The Earhart family encouraged both Amelia and her younger sister, Muriel, to pursue their interests.

Amelia and Muriel lived most of the year with their grandparents, Amelia and Alfred Otis, in Atchison. Mr. Earhart struggled to make a living. He worked for the railroad and he and Mrs. Earhart had to travel a lot.

But Mr. and Mrs. Earhart lived in nearby Kansas City and often visited. They spent summers, family birthdays and holidays together.

One Christmas, seven-year-old Amelia received a boy's sled! A girl's sled was simply a chair on wooden runners. This long wooden boy's sled, with its metal runners, meant Amelia could get a running start, then "belly flop" onto the sled. Now she could build up speed and zoom down the hill, headfirst!

One winter day as she whizzed down
an icy hill, a horse-drawn cart
appeared. It was about to cross her
path. The horse couldn't see Amelia
because of its blinders. The cart driver
couldn't hear her screams. Amelia
couldn't steer well on the ice.

But she could think fast! She lowered
her head and aimed her sled between
the horse's legs. She made it! The boy's
sled saved her! If she had used a girl's
sled and been sitting upright, she'd
have crashed into that horse's belly.

Amelia loved sports as well. But her school, like most in those days, had no teams for girls. Amelia saw neighborhood boys playing basketball. She asked one boy to teach her the game. Soon she had Muriel and their cousins playing on their own backyard basketball team!

When Amelia played sports or searched for insects, she was allowed to wear a new kind of short pant, called bloomers. With those, Amelia jumped and ran freely!

Chapter 2
Hard Times

1907–1919

1908   Ford's Model T car rolls off the assembly line
1912   *Titanic*, the "unsinkable ship," sinks
1914   First traffic lights installed with only red and
        green lights

When she was around ten years old Amelia had to leave her grandparents, her cousins, and Kansas behind. Her father had found a new job with another railroad company. The Earhart family boarded the train and headed for Des Moines, Iowa. Later, Amelia and her family moved many more times.

The Earharts moved a lot because Mr. Earhart began drinking and losing jobs. When Amelia was eighteen the family moved to Chicago. And this time they went without Mr. Earhart. There, Amelia's school had girls' sports teams. But she never joined, because she had to help out at home. But Amelia *always* put on a cheerful face. Even her best friends never knew about her father's drinking or her family's poverty.

After graduating from high school in 1916 Amelia went off by herself to a school in Philadelphia. There she began a scrapbook, which she labeled "Women's Achievement." Inside, Amelia pasted newspaper articles. Each one reported on women who had achieved "firsts."

There were articles about the first women to hold certain positions, such as the president of a bank, the police commissioner, and a city manager. Amelia was becoming more aware of how women could make important contributions to the world.

Two events happened in Amelia's life that allowed her to finally achieve firsts of her own. The first event was in 1903 when Amelia was only six. That's when the Wright brothers built an airplane. Their first flight lasted twelve seconds—quite an achievement then!

The second event was World War I. It started in Europe in 1914. Airplanes had improved by that time and were used in this war. Men were trained to pilot these planes. By 1917 the United States entered the war. Wounded pilots and soldiers came home to recover.

That Christmas Amelia visited Muriel who was at school in Toronto, Canada. Amelia decided to leave school and stay in Toronto to help the many wounded soldiers there. Amelia became a nurse's aide. Some of the men she cared for were pilots.

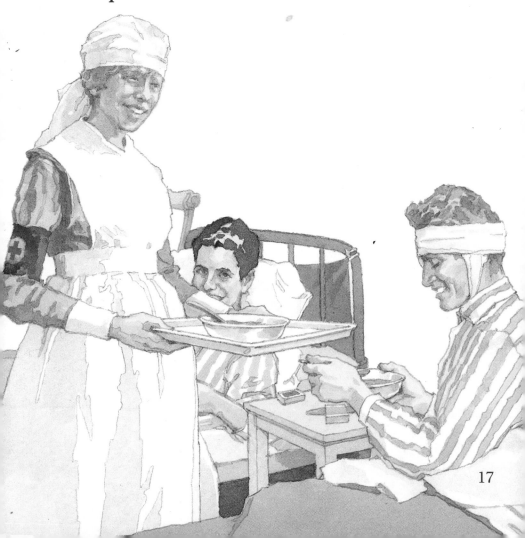

One day Amelia and her girlfriend
went to an airfield to see these pilots fly.
One pilot did the usual loops, rolls,
and spins that pilots did in those days.
But then he aimed his plane low. He
"buzzed" the two young women as they
stood watching. Amelia's friend ran for
cover. Not Amelia.

She said of that day, "I remember the mingled fear and pleasure. . . . I did not understand it at the time, but I believe that little red airplane said something to me as it swished by."

Amelia would have to wait several years to find out just what that plane was saying.

Chapter 3
In The Air!
1920–1928

1920   Women in the U. S. win the right to vote
1921   Bessie Coleman is first African-American *and* first American woman to get pilot's license
1926   Gertrude Ederle is first woman to swim across the English Channel

By the summer of 1920 Amelia went to live with her parents, who were now back together and living in California.

California had a popular weekend activity—air shows. Amelia and her father often watched the former World War I pilots take those planes up into the sky and do their rolls, loops, and spins.

One day Amelia's father bought her a ticket for a ride. Twenty-three-year-old Amelia had her first plane trip—a ten-minute ride over Los Angeles.

Amelia couldn't hold back her excitement. She knew she *had* to fly.

Amelia wanted to take lessons from a woman pilot. Her teacher, Anita Snook, taught Amelia about engine repair as well as flying. After many lessons Amelia finally flew by herself. She was a pilot! Now Amelia wanted to fly all the time. But this sport cost money.

Amelia took a wide variety of jobs—a file clerk, photographer, and truck driver—just to pay for flying time.

For her birthday present the Earharts helped Amelia buy her first plane. It was yellow. Amelia named it *Canary*.

In 1924 Amelia's parents were finally divorcing. Her mother decided to move to Medford, Massachusetts, where Muriel now lived. As usual, money was tight. Amelia sold her plane to buy a car. She needed one to drive herself and her mother across the country. Amelia bought a sports car and named it the *Yellow Peril*.

In Medford, Massachusetts, Amelia got a job at Denison House, a social center in Boston. She taught English to immigrant children who loved piling into the *Yellow Peril* for a ride around the block. Soon Amelia became a social worker at Denison House. For the first time twenty-seven-year-old Amelia found work that she loved.

But on the weekends Amelia rented planes and was in the air! And airplanes and pilots were in the news more and more.

In 1927 Charles Lindbergh was the first person to successfully fly across the Atlantic. Many other pilots wanted the same kind of attention. They wanted to perform a flying first.

LINDBERGH LANDS IN
GREAT OVATION GREETS

One such person was Mrs. Frederick Guest, a rich adventurer. She decided to sponsor a plane trip—one that would carry the first female passenger across the Atlantic. She asked a friend, George Putnam, to find an American woman pilot to be that passenger.

Chapter 4
Amelia's "First"
1928–1932

1926   First commercial airmail flight

1928   First Mickey Mouse cartoon appears

1932   Spelling of Porto Rico changed to Puerto Rico

When Putnam and Amelia met, he knew that she was the perfect choice. Amelia was bright and had a style all her own. Her hair was short. She wore pants, a brown leather jacket, and tied a silken scarf around her neck. Putnam would have an easy time getting the press to write about this beautiful lady pilot.

Wilmer Stultz and Louis Gordon were chosen to fly the plane. Amelia was to make the flying decisions. Mrs. Guest's plane was named *Friendship*. It had pontoons so it could land on water. The *Friendship* took off from East Boston Harbor on Sunday, June 3, 1928. The crew stopped often to refuel. In Newfoundland they were grounded by bad weather and heavy fog.

Finally, fourteen days after starting out, the weather was good—but bad out at sea. Stultz, Gordon, and Earhart decided to take off anyway. The wide Atlantic stretched before them. Soon after takeoff the storm closed in. The captain couldn't fly above the high storm clouds. Snow fell below them. Fog surrounded them. It was a grueling journey.

After more than twenty hours in the air they spotted the coast below. The *Friendship* landed in Burry Port, Wales. They had made it! And Amelia had become her very own first—the first woman to fly across the Atlantic.

Crowds in Europe cheered them. They sailed back to New York and got a ticker-tape parade. Amelia wrote articles and books about her adventure. Amelia wanted to go back to social work. But flying and giving speeches about her experiences took up too much of her time.

Amelia also wanted to do *exactly* what Lindbergh had done—fly solo across the Atlantic. She studied maps and charts to prepare for the trip.

Amelia left Newfoundland on May 20, 1932. Four hours from land Amelia was in real trouble. It was dark. She was flying in a storm and her equipment was failing. She couldn't tell how high she was flying. The reserve gas tank leaked, and gas dripped down her neck.

Earhart Makes Perfect Start on Solo Sea Flight

The electrical storm tossed her
plane. Amelia tried to climb above the
storm. But ice formed on her wings.
For a time her plane spun out of
control. She tried lowering her plane.
The ice on the wings melted. Yes! But
now she was about to hit the sea's
swelling waves! No! Throughout the
flight, Amelia battled the storm.

Finally Amelia saw land. But she
didn't know how much fuel she had left.
She picked the nearest spot that gave
her the safest landing. It was a cow
pasture. After she landed Amelia asked
the man standing there, "Where am I?"
He told her she was near Londonderry,
Ireland. He couldn't believe she'd come
all the way from America!

Amelia phoned Putnam, whom she had married in 1931. Within hours the world got the news—Amelia Earhart was the first woman to fly solo across the Atlantic! Amelia had achieved the first she had longed for.

Chapter 5
The Final Flight

1937

1937	*Snow White and the Seven Dwarfs* is first feature-length animated movie
1939	George Putnam's book, *Soaring Wings*, a biography of Amelia, is published
1941	On December 7, Pearl Harbor, Hawaii, is bombed; United States enters World War II

Now Amelia was known all over the world! She was honored first by President Coolidge, then President Hoover. She became a close friend of President Franklin Roosevelt and his wife, Eleanor.

Amelia Earhart, First Woman to Fly the Atlantic, talks about the status of women with First Lady, Eleanor Roosevelt.

But above all, Amelia kept accomplishing her own firsts.

She helped create the first women's flying club and became its first president. It was called the Ninety-Nines because it had ninety-nine founding members. Beside other flying firsts, Amelia also had luggage named after her and designed a line of women's clothing.

Miss Amelia Earhart
"Lady Lindy"—the First Woman to Fly the Atlantic
AND
George Palmer Putnam
Explorer, Boy Scout Enthusiast
Publisher
COAT DESIGNED BY MISS EARHART

When Amelia was almost forty years old, she decided to fly around the world! She selected her plane and her navigator, Fred Noonan. Amelia studied maps and charts and planned her route. The plane was fitted with a new tool: a radio that transmitted and received signals.

Amelia and Fred left on June 1, 1937, from Miami, Florida. They headed east. At each stop she was in contact with her husband. Amelia and Fred were greeted warmly at each place they stopped along the way.

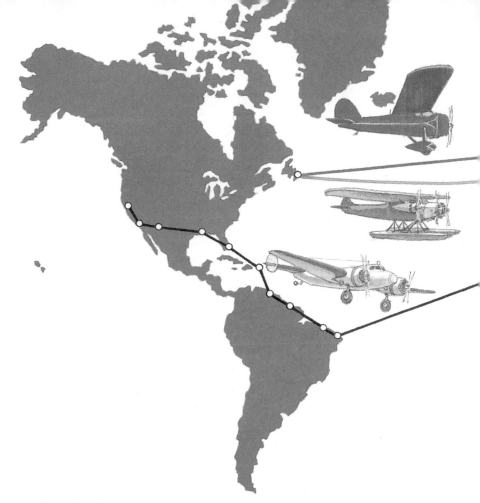

On July 2 Amelia and Fred took off
from Lae, in New Guinea. She was due
to land on Howland Island in the Pacific
Ocean. But her radio was not working
well. The ground crew lost contact.
There was no sign that her plane ever
landed on the island. There was no sign
that the plane crashed into the ocean.

There was no trace of Amelia, Fred, or the plane. Amelia Earhart was gone! Amelia Earhart's disappearance was a mystery. Some people believe she simply ran out of fuel. Others believed she was a spy for the United States and had been captured. No one really knows what happened to her.

Amelia Earhart is one of the most famous aviators in the world. And she was an unsung feminist during her life. Amelia Earhart never felt that she *should not* or *could not* do something, simply because she was a woman. And with her fame she inspired young girls to dream.

Amelia Earhart said it best: "To enjoy doing something, to concentrate all of your energy on it—that is not only the surest guarantee of its success. It is also being true to yourself."

Here is a timeline of Amelia Earhart's life:

1897   Amelia is born in Atchison, Kansas, on July 24

1899   Sister, Muriel, born on December 29

1918   Becomes a nurse's aide in Toronto, Ontario, Canada

1920   Takes her first airplane ride

1921–22   Takes her first flying lesson, buys her first plane, and gets her pilot's license

1924   Parents divorce; Amelia moves to Massachusetts

1926   Becomes a social worker at Denison House in Boston

1928   First woman to fly across the Atlantic; the trip takes 20 Hours and 40 minutes

1928   President Calvin Coolidge honors Earhart, Stultz, and Gordon at the White House

1929   Helps start a woman's pilot club, the Ninety-Nines

1930   Sets women's speed record, 181.18 miles per hour

1931   Marries George Putnam

1932   First woman to fly solo across the Atlantic; trip takes 14 hours and 54 minutes

1932   President Herbert Hoover presents her with National Geographic Society's Gold Medal

1935   First person to fly solo from Honolulu, Hawaii, to Oakland, California; from Los Angeles to Mexico City; and the first person to fly nonstop from Mexico City to Newark, New Jersey

1937   Attempts to fly around the world with Fred Noonan; after completing 22,000 miles, or two-thirds of her total flight, her plane disappears

1937   Amelia Earhart declared dead on July 16

DATE			